Mastering Binary Trading:
A Comprehensive Guide to Success

Explanation of binary trading and its appeal
The importance of education and risk
management
Overview of what the book will cover

Chapter 1: Understanding Binary Options

1. Basic Concept: Binary trading is based on a simple yes/no proposition. Traders speculate on whether the price of a particular asset, such as a currency pair, stock, commodity, or index, will rise or fall within a specified time frame. They have two options:

- Call Option: If a trader believes the price will go up, they choose a "call" option.
- Put Option: If a trader believes the price will go down, they choose a "put" option.

1. Comparison to traditional trading Benefits and risks

One of the primary appeals of binary trading is the fixed payout structure. Before placing a trade, traders know exactly how much they stand to gain or lose. If their prediction is correct at the expiration of the option, they receive a predetermined payout, typically in the range of 70-90% of their initial investment. If they are wrong, they lose the initial investment amount.

2. Short Time Frames:

Binary options have short time frames, ranging from seconds to minutes (short-term) or days (long-term). This appeals to traders who prefer quick results and don't want to tie up their capital for extended periods.

3. Fixed Payouts:

One of the primary appeals of binary trading is the fixed payout structure. Before placing a trade, traders know exactly how much they stand to gain or lose. If their prediction is correct at the expiration of the option, they receive a predetermined payout, typically in the range of 70-90% of their initial investment. If they are wrong, they lose the initial investment amount.

4. Simplicity:

Binary trading is straight forward, making it accessible to both beginners and experienced traders. There are no complex calculations or margin requirements. Traders only need to predict the direction of price movement.

5. Limited Risk:

Traders know their potential loss upfront, which helps in managing risk. They cannot lose more than their initial investment, unlike some other forms of trading where losses can exceed the initial capital.

6. Asset Variety:

Binary options cover a wide range of underlying assets, including currencies, commodities, stocks, and indices. This variety allows traders to diversify their portfolio

Commodities—-------Oil, Wheat, silver, Gold

7. Accessibility:

Binary trading platforms are easily accessible online, and many brokers offer user-friendly interfaces. Traders can access these platforms 24/7, providing flexibility to trade at their convenience.

8. Lower Capital Requirement:

Compared to traditional stock trading, binary options require lower capital to get started. Traders can start with small investments and gradually increase their positions as they gain experience.

9. Hedging Opportunities:

Binary options can also be used for hedging purposes. Traders can protect their existing investments by using binary options to offset potential losses in other markets.

10. Market Volatility Opportunities:

The short-term nature of binary options allows traders to profit from even small price movements in highly volatile markets, which can be challenging for traditional traders.

While binary trading offers these advantages, it's essential to remember that it carries substantial risks. The fixed payout structure also means that losses can accumulate quickly if predictions are incorrect. Therefore, individuals interested in binary trading should educate themselves, develop a solid trading strategy, and practice responsible risk management to maximize their chances of success.

Chapter 2: Getting Started

HERE WE WILL LEARN HOW TO

1. SET UP A TRADING PLATFORM
2. CHOOSE A RELIABLE BROKER
3. DEPOSITS
4. WITHDRAWALS
5. DEMO TRADING FOR PRACTICE

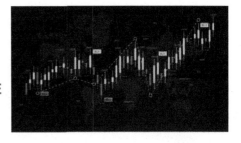

1. SET UP A TRADING PLATFORM

THERE ARE SEVERAL TRADING PLACES TO TRADE

THESE ARE THE TOP 5

1. TRADINGVIEW
2. WEBULL
3. NINJA TRADER
4. E-TRADE
5. FIDELITY

2. CHOOSING A RELIABLE BROKER

Choosing a reliable broker is crucial for your trading success and the safety of your investments. Here are some key factors to consider when selecting a reliable broker

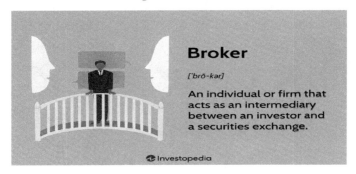

1. Regulation and Licensing:

Ensure the broker is regulated by a reputable financial authority or regulatory body in your country or region. Regulatory oversight helps protect your funds and ensures fair trading practices.

2. Security and Safety:

Verify the broker's security measures, including data encryption, firewall protection, and client fund segregation. Your funds should be held in separate accounts from the broker's operational funds.

3. Reputation and Track Record:

Research the broker's history and reputation. Look for reviews, testimonials, and feedback from other traders. A long-established and well-regarded broker is often a safer choice.

4. Trading Fees and Commissions:

Understand the broker's fee structure, including spreads, commissions, overnight financing charges, and any other fees. Compare these fees with other brokers to ensure they are competitive.

5. Trading Platforms:

Evaluate the trading platform offered by the broker. It should be user-friendly, stable, and offer the features and tools you need for your trading style

6. Asset Coverage:

Ensure the broker offers access to the financial markets and asset classes you intend to trade, such as stocks, forex, commodities, cryptocurrencies, or options.

7. Customer Support:

Test the broker's customer support by contacting them with questions or issues. Reliable brokers offer responsive and helpful customer service through various channels, such as live chat, phone, or email.

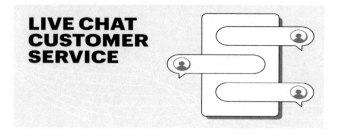

8. Account Types and Minimum Deposits:

Check if the broker offers account types that suit your trading needs and budget. Be wary of brokers with excessively high minimum deposit requirements.

9. Deposit and Withdrawal Options:

Verify the availability of convenient and secure deposit and withdrawal methods. Ensure the broker allows hassle-free transactions.

10. Educational Resources:

Look for brokers that provide educational materials, webinars, tutorials, and market analysis to help you improve your trading skills.

11. Trading Tools and Research:

Assess the quality and quantity of research tools and analysis resources offered by the broker. Reliable brokers often provide access to real-time news, charts, and economic calendars.

12. Transparency and Disclosure:

Ensure the broker is transparent about its policies, terms, and conditions. Read the fine print, especially concerning fees, withdrawals, and trading conditions.

13. Demo Account:

Before committing real capital, use a broker's demo account to practice and get a feel for the trading platform.

THE RULE OF THUMB IS IF YOU CAN WIN 25 TRADES IN

A ROW THEN YOU ARE READY FOR THE LIVE TRADE

14. Client Reviews and Recommendations:

Seek out reviews and recommendations from other traders, but be cautious of fake reviews. Forums and social media groups can also provide insights into a broker's reputation.

15. Regulatory Alerts:

Stay informed about any regulatory warnings or actions against the broker. Regulators often publish alerts about unscrupulous brokers.

Remember that your choice of broker should align with your trading goals, risk tolerance, and experience level. It's essential to conduct thorough research, read the broker's terms and conditions carefully, and start with a small deposit or demo account before committing significant capital to any broker.

Chapter 3: Market Analysis

THERE ARE 3 TYPES OF MARKET ANALYSIS

1. **Fundamental Analysis:**
2. **Technical Analysis:**
3. **Sentiment Analysis:**

1. Fundamental Analysis:

What It Involves: Fundamental analysis focuses on assessing the intrinsic value of an asset by examining the underlying economic, financial, and qualitative factors that affect its price. This analysis typically involves studying financial statements, economic indicators, news events, and industry trends.

Key Components:

- Earnings reports: Analyzing a company's financial performance, including revenue, earnings, and profit margins.
- Balance sheets: Assessing assets, liabilities, and equity to gauge financial health.
- Economic indicators: Monitoring economic data such as GDP growth, employment figures, and inflation rates.
- Industry analysis: Evaluating the industry's growth prospects and competitive dynamics.

Use Cases:

Fundamental analysis is often used for long-term investing in stocks, bonds, and commodities. It can help investors identify undervalued or overvalued assets and make decisions based on a company's financial health and growth potential.

2. Technical Analysis:

What It Involves: Technical analysis focuses on studying historical price and volume data of assets to forecast future price movements. It assumes that historical price patterns and trends will repeat themselves.

Key Components:

- Price charts: Analyzing price patterns, trends, and support/resistance levels on price charts.
- Technical indicators: Using tools like moving averages, relative strength index (RSI), and stochastic oscillators to identify potential buy or sell signals.
- Volume analysis: Examining trading volumes to confirm or invalidate price movements.

Use Cases:

Technical analysis is commonly used in short- to medium-term trading across various asset classes, including stocks, forex, cryptocurrencies, and commodities. Traders use technical analysis to identify entry and exit points and to set stop-loss and take-profit levels.

3. Sentiment Analysis:

What It Involves: Sentiment analysis gauges market sentiment and investor psychology by studying factors like news, social media, and market sentiment indicators. It aims to understand the collective mood of market participants.

Key Components:

- News and events: Analyzing how news events and economic releases impact market sentiment.
- Social media sentiment: Tracking social media discussions and sentiment about specific assets or the market as a whole.
- Market sentiment indicators: Using tools like the put/call ratio and the VIX (volatility index) to assess market sentiment extremes.

Use Cases:

Sentiment analysis can be valuable for short-term trading and identifying contrarian opportunities. It helps traders gauge whether the market is overly optimistic (bullish) or pessimistic (bearish) and make decisions accordingly.

In practice, traders and investors often combine elements of all three types of analysis to form a well-rounded view of the market. The choice of analysis method depends on individual preferences, trading style, and the asset class being traded. Additionally, risk management, portfolio diversification, and staying updated on current events are essential aspects of successful market analysis and trading.

Chapter 4 Trading Strategies

Trading strategies are systematic plans or approaches that traders use to make informed decisions about buying or selling assets in financial markets. These strategies are designed to provide a structured and disciplined approach to trading and aim to increase the probability of making profitable trades. Here are some common trading strategies:

1. Trend Following:

Description: Trend-following strategies involve identifying and trading in the direction of prevailing market trends. Traders use technical indicators and price patterns to confirm and follow established trends.

Trend Trading

Indicators used:

Moving averages, Relative Strength Index (RSI), Moving Average Convergence Divergence (MACD), and trendlines.

We will go over indicators in a later chapter

2. Swing Trading:

Description: Swing traders aim to capture shorter to medium-term price movements within a trend. They look for opportunities to enter trades at swing highs and lows and aim to profit from price swings.

Indicators used:

- **Technical analysis indicators, chart patterns, and support/resistance levels.**

3. Day Trading:

Description: Day traders buy and sell assets within the same trading day, closing all positions by the market close. They aim to profit from short-term price fluctuations and market volatility.

Strategies:

Scalping (very short-term trades), momentum trading, and arbitrage.

4. Range Trading:

Description: Range traders identify periods when an asset's price is trading within a defined range or channel. They buy near support levels and sell near resistance levels.

Indicators used:

Support and resistance levels, Bollinger Bands, and oscillators.

A Complete Guide to
Understanding **Bollinger Bands**

5. Breakout Trading:

Description: Breakout traders look for opportunities when an asset's price breaks out of a well-defined trading range. They seek to capitalize on sharp price movements that follow a breakout.

Breakout Trading Strategy

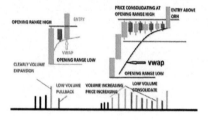

6. Contrarian Trading:

Description: Contrarian traders go against prevailing market sentiment. They buy when sentiment is excessively bearish and sell when it's excessively bullish, assuming that market sentiment will eventually reverse.

Indicators used:

Sentiment indicators, such as the put/call ratio or the Volatility Index (VIX).

7. Algorithmic Trading:

Description: Algorithmic trading involves using computer programs and algorithms to automate trading decisions based on predefined rules. These strategies can range from high-frequency trading to long-term investment algorithms.

Algorithmic Trading

Example

Programmer — Develop → Code

Assesses market situation dynamically

Saves time for trader

WallStreetMojo

Indicators used:

Programming languages (Python, C++, etc.), trading platforms, and historical data

8. Position Trading:

Description: Position traders take a long-term perspective and hold positions for weeks, months, or even years. They base their trades on fundamental analysis and longer-term trends.

Indicators used:

Fundamental analysis, economic indicators, and global events.

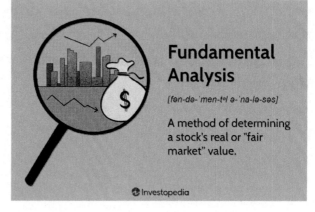

9. Options Trading Strategies:

Description: Options traders use a variety of strategies, such as covered calls, straddles, strangles, and spreads, to profit from the movement or lack of movement in the underlying asset's price.

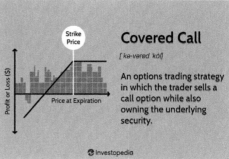

Indicators used:

Options contracts, implied volatility, and options pricing models.

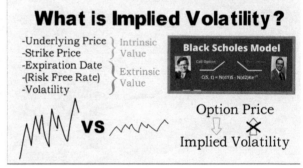

10. Carry Trading:

Description: Carry traders aim to profit from the interest rate differential between two currencies. They borrow funds in a currency with a low-interest rate and invest in a currency with a higher interest rate.

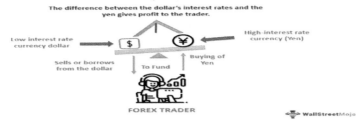

Analysis:

Interest rate differentials and economic stability of the countries involved.

Interest Rate Differential Meaning

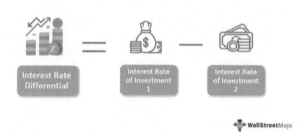

It's important to note that no single trading strategy guarantees success, and each strategy has its own set of risks. Traders often combine multiple strategies, employ strict risk management rules, and adapt their approach to changing market conditions. Additionally, thorough backtesting and continuous learning are essential for refining and improving trading strategies over time.

CHAPTER 5 RISK MANAGEMENT

RISK MANAGEMENT IS PROBABLY THE HARDEST OBSTACLE TRADERS FACE. LOSING MONEY IS NEVER A GOOD THING WHEN TRADING BINARY OPTIONS. BUT WITH A LITTLE DISCIPLINE AND PATIENCE YOU CAN OBTAIN YOUR TRADES PROFITABLY

Risk management is a critical component of successful trading and investing. It involves strategies and techniques to mitigate potential losses and protect your capital. Effective risk management is essential for preserving your trading account and ensuring long-term profitability. Here are key principles and strategies for risk management:

1. Position Sizing:

- Determine the size of each position based on your overall capital and risk tolerance. Avoid risking a significant portion of your capital on a single trade.
- Use the "2% rule," which suggests risking no more than 2% of your total capital on a single trade. Adjust this percentage based on your risk tolerance and the trade's probability of success.

2. Stop Loss Orders:

- Place stop-loss orders for every trade to limit potential losses. A stop loss is an order to sell an asset when it reaches a specific price level. It ensures that you exit a losing trade before the losses become excessive.
- Set stop-loss levels based on technical analysis, support and resistance levels, or your predefined risk tolerance.

3. Take Profit Orders:

- Similarly, use take-profit orders to lock in profits at a predetermined price level. Taking profits helps you avoid potential reversals that could erase your gains.
- Set take-profit levels based on technical analysis, resistance levels, or your profit target.

4. Risk-Reward Ratio:

- Before entering a trade, assess the risk-reward ratio. This ratio compares the potential profit (reward) to the potential loss (risk).
- A common rule of thumb is to seek trades with a risk-reward ratio of at least 1:2 or 1:3. This means you are willing to risk $1 to make $2 or $3.

5. Diversification:

- Avoid overconcentration in a single asset or asset class. Diversify your portfolio to spread risk across various investments. A well-diversified portfolio can reduce the impact of a single losing trade.
- Diversification can include different asset types, industries, and geographic regions

6. Risk Tolerance:

- Assess your risk tolerance honestly. Understand how much risk you are comfortable taking and adjust your trading strategies accordingly.
- Avoid taking excessive risks that can lead to emotional stress and impulsive decision-making.

7. Use Leverage Cautiously:

- If you use leverage, do so with caution. While leverage can amplify gains, it can also magnify losses.
- Make sure you fully understand how leverage works and its potential impact on your account.

8. Risk Management Plan:

- Develop a comprehensive risk management plan that outlines your strategies for managing risk. Include guidelines for position sizing, stop losses, take profits, and risk-reward ratios.
- Stick to your plan consistently, even when emotions run high.

9. Continuous Monitoring and Adaptation:

- Monitor your trades regularly and be prepared to adjust stop-loss and take-profit levels as market conditions change.
- Reevaluate and update your risk management plan periodically to reflect your evolving trading experience and risk tolerance.

10. Emotional Discipline:

Control your emotions, particularly fear and greed, which can lead to impulsive decisions and poor risk management. - Maintain discipline in following your risk management rules, even when faced with market volatility.

*******IMPORTANT*******

Effective risk management is a fundamental aspect of trading and investing that can help protect your capital and keep you in the game for the long term. It's crucial to prioritize risk management alongside your trading strategies and continually refine your approach based on your experience and market conditions.

CHAPTER 6:   TRADING INDICATORS

Trading indicators are tools and mathematical calculations used by traders and investors to analyze financial markets and make informed trading decisions. These indicators provide insights into price trends, momentum, volatility, and other aspects of market behavior. There are numerous trading indicators available, and traders often use a combination of them to develop trading strategies. Here are some commonly used trading indicators:

1. MOVING AVERAGE

THERE ARE TWO MOVING AVERAGES

1. **Simple Moving Average (SMA):**
2. **Exponential Moving Average (EMA):**

2. Relative Strength Index (RSI):

RSI measures the strength and speed of price movements. It ranges from 0 to 100 and helps identify overbought (above 70) and oversold (below 30) conditions.

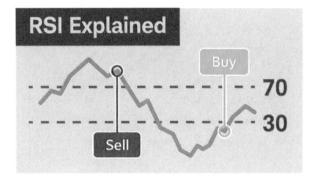

3. Moving Average Convergence Divergence (MACD):

MACD is a trend-following momentum indicator that shows the relationship between two moving averages of an asset's price. It helps identify potential trend reversals.

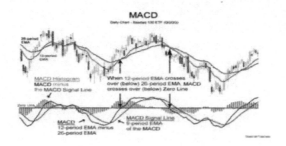

4. Stochastic Oscillator:

The stochastic oscillator measures the momentum of an asset relative to its price range over a specified period. It generates values between 0 and 100, helping traders identify overbought and oversold conditions.

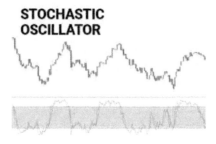

STOCHASTIC
OSCILLATOR

5. Bollinger Bands:

Bollinger Bands consist of a middle band (SMA) and two outer bands representing standard deviations from the middle band. They help identify volatility and potential price reversals

A Complete Guide to Understanding **Bollinger Bands**

6. Fibonacci Retracement:

Fibonacci retracement levels are horizontal lines on a price chart that indicate potential support and resistance levels based on Fibonacci ratios. Traders use them to identify price retracement levels in a trend.

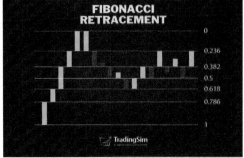

7. Ichimoku Cloud:

The Ichimoku Cloud is a comprehensive indicator that provides information on support and resistance levels, trend direction, and potential entry and exit points.

8. Average True Range (ATR):

ATR measures market volatility by calculating the average range between the high and low prices over a specific period. Traders use it to set stop-loss levels and position sizes.

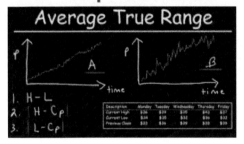

9. Volume Profile:

Volume profile displays the volume of trading at different price levels, helping traders identify areas of support and resistance and potential price reversals.

10. Parabolic SAR (Stop and Reverse):

Parabolic SAR places dots above or below the price chart to indicate potential trend reversals. When the dots switch from above to below the price, it suggests a bullish trend, and vice versa.

11. On-Balance Volume (OBV):

OBV measures buying and selling pressure based on trading volume. It helps identify potential trend reversals by comparing volume to price movements.

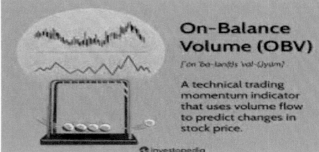

12. Williams % R:

Williams %R is a momentum oscillator that measures overbought and oversold conditions. It ranges from -100 to 0, with readings below -80 indicating oversold conditions and readings above -20 indicating overbought conditions.

******IMPORTANT******

Traders should carefully choose indicators that align with their trading style, goals, and the assets they trade. It's also essential to avoid overloading charts with too many indicators, as this can lead to confusion. A thorough understanding of how each indicator works and how they complement each other is crucial for effective technical analysis. Additionally, indicators should be used in conjunction with other forms of analysis, such as fundamental analysis and risk management, to make well-informed trading decisions.

CHAPTER 7: CANDLE STYLES

THERE ARE NINE CANDLE STYLES TO TRADE WITH

1. REGULAR CANDLES
2. HEIKIN ASHI
3. HOLLOW
4. LINE
5. LINE WITH MARKERS
6. STEP LINE
7. BASE LINE
8. COLUMN
9. RENKO

REGULAR CANDLES

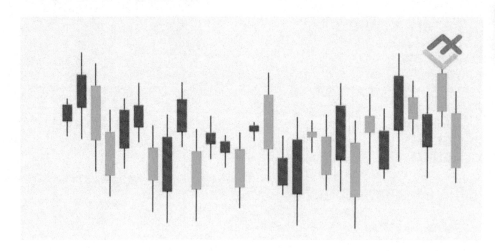

HEIKIN ASHI

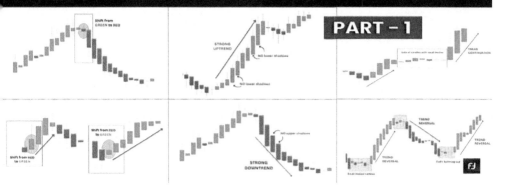

HOLLOW CANDLES

Irrespective of the candle's color:

current candle's close
is greater than
current candle's open

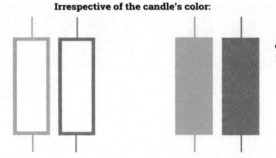

current candle's close
is lesser than current
candle's open

FILL OF HOLLOW CANDLES

The fill of a hollow candle is decided by comparing the close of the current candle
with the open of the current candle

● ● ●

LINE TRADING CANDLES

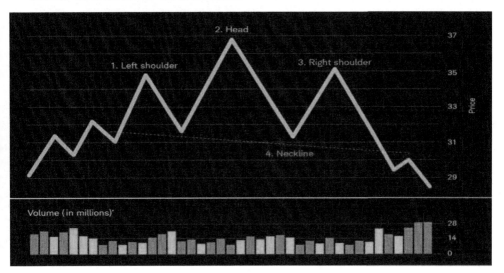

LINE WITH MARKERS

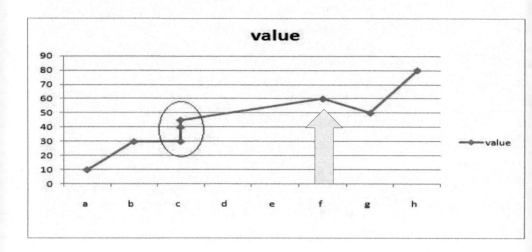

STEP LINE

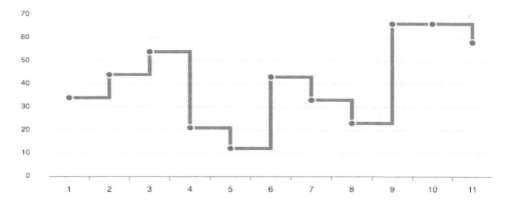

BASE LINE

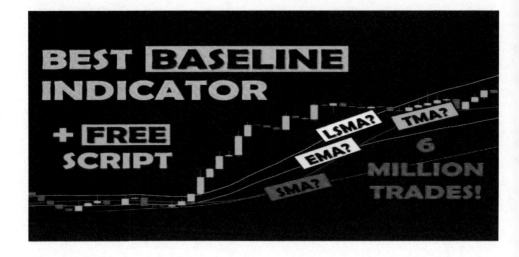

COLUMN TRADING CANDLE

RENKO CANDLES

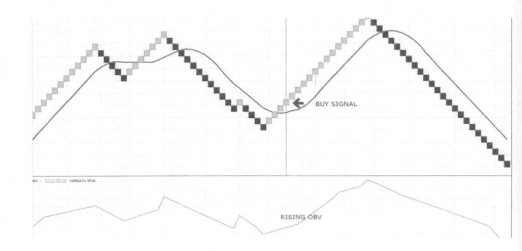

*******IMPORTANT*******

IT'S IMPORTANT TO KEEP IN MIND THAT NOT ALL
CANDLE FORMS MAY WORK FOR YOU
EXPERIMENT AND TRY EACH ONE TO YOUR LIKING
AND COMFORT ZONE

SUMMARIZING

THE TAKE AWAY FROM THIS GUIDE IS THAT TRADE SMARTLY AND CAUTIOUSLY. TAKE YOUR TIME AND ANALYZE EACH TRADE . MORE YOU USE A DEMO ACCOUNT THE BETTER YOU WILL GET AND BE ABLE TO TRANSITION TO LIVE TRADING. LEARN EACH INDICATOR FOR THEY CAN GUIDE YOU TO A PROFITABLE TRADE

GLOSSARY OF TERMS

1. Binary Options:

- Financial contracts that allow traders to predict the direction of an asset's price movement within a specified time frame. Payouts are fixed and predetermined.

2. Call Option:

- A binary option that predicts the price of the underlying asset will rise before the option's expiration time.

3. Put Option:

- A binary option that predicts the price of the underlying asset will fall before the option's expiration time.

4. Strike Price (Exercise Price):

- The price at which a binary option can be exercised. It determines whether the option will be "in the money" or "out of the money" at expiration.

5. Expiration Time (Expiry):

- The predetermined time at which a binary option contract expires. Traders must make their predictions before this time.

6. In the Money (ITM):

- A binary option that has reached a profitable outcome for the trader. For a call option, it means the asset's price is higher than the strike price at expiration. For a put option, it means the asset's price is lower.

7. Out of the Money (OTM):

- A binary option that has resulted in a loss for the trader. For a call option, it means the asset's price is lower than the strike price at expiration. For a put option, it means the asset's price is higher

8. At the Money (ATM):

- A binary option in which the asset's price is approximately equal to the strike price at expiration. It doesn't result in a profit or loss.

9. Payout (Return):

- The fixed amount a trader receives if their binary option expires in the money. The payout is determined at the beginning of the trade.
-

10. Risk-Reward Ratio: - The ratio between the potential profit (reward) and potential loss (risk) of a binary option trade. It helps traders assess the trade's attractiveness.

11. Broker: - A financial institution or platform that offers binary options trading services to traders. Brokers facilitate the trading process and provide access to markets.

12. Underlying Asset: - The financial instrument or asset on which a binary option is based, such as a currency pair, stock, commodity, or index.

13. High/Low Option: - The simplest type of binary option where traders predict whether the price of the underlying asset will be higher or lower than the strike price at expiration.

14. Boundary (Range) Option: - A binary option where traders predict whether the price of the underlying asset will remain within a specified price range or break out of that range at expiration.

15. One-Touch Option: - A binary option where traders predict whether the price of the underlying asset will touch or exceed a specified price level at least once before expiration.

16. Double No-Touch Option: - A binary option where traders predict that the price of the underlying asset will not touch or exceed two specified price levels before expiration.

17. Early Closure (Buyout): - A feature offered by some brokers that allows traders to exit a binary option trade before its scheduled expiration time. This feature can help manage losses or lock in profits.

18. Roll-Over: - A feature offered by some brokers that allows traders to extend the expiration time of a binary option for an additional fee, giving the trade more time to become profitable.

Understanding these binary options terms is essential for anyone looking to engage in binary options trading. It's important to thoroughly research and understand the specific terms and conditions of the broker you choose to trade with, as these may vary among different brokers.

About the Author

HI MY NAME IS MARK INLOW RETIRED NAVY VETERAN I HAVE BEEN TRADING BINARY OPTIONS FOR 7 YEARS NOW AND I DESIGNED THIS GUIDE TO HELP NEW AND NOVICE TRADERS TO LEARN THE FUN AND EXCITING WORLD OF BINARY TRADING I HOPE THIS BOOK HELPS AND LET THE TRADING BEGIN

Printed in Great Britain
by Amazon

32572374R00059